Preserving Everything

Effortless Ball Canning Recipes. Make Home Canning and Preserving Easy. Save all the Nutritions in a proper way

Lavina Winslow

DISCLAIMER NOTICE

Please note the information contained in this document is for educational and entertainment purposes only. All effort has been executed to present accurate, up-to-date, and reliable, complete information. No warranties of any kind are declared or implied. Readers acknowledge that the author is not engaging in legal, financial, medical, or professional rendering before attempting any techniques outlined in this book.

By reading this document, the reader agrees that under no circumstances is the author responsible for any losses, direct or indirect, which are incurred as a result of the use of the information contained in this document, including, but not limited to, - errors, omissions, or inaccuracies

@ copyright- All rights reserved.

TABLE OF CONTENTS

RECIPES

INTRODUCTION

This book is intended for the beginning, as well as the experienced, canner who wants to extend the pleasures of pickling, preserving, and making unusual taste treats of all sorts in small batches during any time of the year. A good portion of the recipes can be refrigerated instead of being sealed in jars, which is a boon especially in the winter months when canning supplies are often difficult to find. All of these recipes will provide you with tasty and unusual treats that are perfect to give as gifts. It should be noted that many of the recipes can be safely altered to reflect your own indi- vidual taste and preferences. I hope you enjoy expanding your canning and preserving experiences through these small-batch recipes.

FOOD PRESERVATION

History of Food Preservation

The need for food preservation has existed for as long as people have. It has not, however, always been as foolproof as the options available today. To be sure, the road to developing safe, predictable methods of preserv- ing foods is littered with illness, worthless food, and even death. Thankfully, we get to reap the knowledge learned in the past. And if we use this information wisely, we can avoid repeating those mistakes.

Most areas of our world cannot be harvested all year. Nor is it wise to hunt all year even if your chosen prey is available. So, how do we feed ourselves in the "off-season"? We must prepare for these times, as they are most certainly coming. Food planning became more than going over the hill to see if the berry bushes were ripe yet. Over time people developed ways of preserving food.

Dehydration, it was found, eliminated the moisture content of meats, fruits, herbs, and vegetables. This moisture was, in part, the cause of these foods to rot. Thinly sliced and hung or laid out in the sun to dry was the simplest means of food preservation. Salting, brining, and smoking followed. All of these methods were inexpensive and simple enough that each household was able to care for its own needs. As science progressed, bacteria and enzymes, and their effects on foods were discovered; preventions were learned. If food was brought up to a certain temperature, and then sealed in air and moisture resistant containers, removing any air in the container during the process, it could be stored for great periods of time. "Canning," as this convenience was known, was invented. Following World War II, as the electrical grid came to even the furthest out-lying farms and ranches, and prices for various metals came down with the increase of industrial- ization, freezing food became a reliable method of food preservation. Although the canning process is the most labor intensive procedure, all methods promote a sense of pride, accomplishment, and self-reliance. There's nothing like opening the pantry or freezer door on a frigid winter's day, where the snow – already up to the window sills – is coming down so hard you can't see your mailbox, and finding row upon row of neatly labeled produce and meats and remembering once again that if the world ended outside your door, your family would still eat well.

Definition of Preservation Methods

Canning

– Processing food in airtight containers for preservation. This process uses containers made of alu- minum, tin, or glass. Hot food is packed into the container and sealed either under pressure or a boiling water bath.

Dehydration

– Simply put, removing the water from food products for preservation. In early history, food was thinly sliced and placed on flat rocks in the sun to dry. Later, as people became less nomadic, racks were built for hanging long, thin slices of meat, think of jerky. Commercially purchased dehydrators utilize mesh screens for racks, and electric fans to continually pull air across the food. The mesh screens allow the air to reach both sides of the food, while the fan speeds the process. Bacteria must have moisture to grow and multiply. Eliminating the moisture in food eliminates the bacteria that cause spoilage.

Dry-Salting

– This process draws moisture from food using a great deal of salt. This moisture dissolves the salt into brine, which inhibits the growth of micro-organisms. Only small or thin foods can be preserved this way. Small fish are often preserved in this manner. Done properly, fish can then be refrigerated for as long as two years.

Fermentation

– Although very similar to brining, fermentation requires very exacting measurements of salt, vinegar, and temperature. Caused by benign micro-organisms interacting with salt brine, they convert vegetable sugars into acids. Dill pickles are made in this method, which can take three to six weeks to prepare. If processed (using pressure canning) following the fermentation period, these foods can be kept indefinitely.

Freezing

– Placing protected food in an environment that keeps it at 0oF [-18oC]. This method of food preservation is the easiest. It also keeps most foods closest to their

original form. Not including the original investment in the actual appliance, freezing is a very economical way of preserving food. A quick blanch to halt enzyme production, and protection from the frigid, dry air is all that is required in preparation.

Jelling

– Preserving with sugar seems to be a contradiction in terms. It is true that micro-organisms thrive on weak sugar solu- tion. In a strong concentration sugar has a dehydrating effect, similar to that of salt, inhibiting the development of micro-organisms. When pectin is added, the fruit being preserved gels, or jel- lies. Jellies, jams, marmalades, and preserves are all made with similar processes. They are then put in sterile containers, sealed with paraffin, and stored in a cool, dry environment. Only fruit butters, cheeses, and preserves of whole fruit pieces should instead be water bath processed.

Irradiation

– Although not available to the in-home food preserver, this method of preservation is being utilized more frequently as the technology improves. In its simplest defini- tion, food is exposed to a dose of ionizing radiation. The dose of radiation and time of exposure varies. This process works by damaging the microbe's DNA in such a way as it is unable to repair it. When this occurs, the microbe cannot mature, nor can it process cell division, its method of reproduction. If the dosage is high enough, the microbe is killed outright. Although the food itself cannot become radioactive (the particles transmitting the radiation are not themselves radioactive), and this method of food preservation is used in more than fifty countries worldwide, because of its association with the nuclear industry, some people in the USA still find food irradiation to be controversial.

Pickling – Also called brining, this method infuses wonderful flavors into the food being preserved. Brine is made, usually containing salt, sugar, and vinegar. Herbs or other flavoring ingredients are added to the brine and then heated. The food being preserved is then immersed in the brine. Ice can be used to prevent any fermentation from occurring. Depending on the food being preserved and the amount of flavor to be infused, brining times can be as little as fifteen min- utes or as long as months.

Smoking – In the same way dehydration preserves meats, smoking also depletes it of moisture. However, the aroma of the wood smoke is absorbed by the meat, flavoring it in a way that cannot be otherwise duplicated. From lightly scented maple wood to the heady flavors derived from the smoke of oak or hickory, the choice of wood is a great consideration for the end product desired.

Smoking times can vary from just a few hours to a week or more. Meats preserved this way do require refrigeration. Smoking may also be used in conjunction with salting or brining.

Equipment

Most of the recipes in this collection can easily be made with equipment already in your kitchen but you may want to add a few tools as you go along.

Below is a list of the most commonly needed equipment in order to successfully can and preserve just about everything in this book:

- Measuring spoons—metal works best.

- Measuring cups in 1-, 2-, and 4-cup sizes—glass is handiest for measuring liquids and can go in the microwave if necessary. Metal cups are good for sugar and solids.

- Tongs—used to remove boiled jars and lids from boiling water.

- Wide-mouthed funnel—to fit a standard canning jar, preferably metal.

- Sharp knives—buy the best you can afford and also a good sharpener.

- Spoons—an assortment of wood and metal; a flat- ended wooden spoon is a great help when stirring a hot bubbling pot, and a slotted spoon is also useful for straining.

- For breaking up hard spices, such as cinnamon sticks and pepper corns, a tool such as a metal meat- tenderizing mallet will help. A hammer covered with a cloth will work too.

- Vegetable brush—keep it just for food use.

- Grater—one with a variety of hole sizes.

- Juicer

- Ladle for filling jars—a long-handled measuring cup or a teacup will work as a substitute but remember, it will get hot.

- Jar lid tightener—a variety of them is on the market from a useful nonslip pad to a metal gripper.

- Hot pads

- Dishcloths

- Hand and dish towels

- Apron—boiling kettles do spit and fruit juices will stain your clothing.

- Paper towels

- Cheesecloth or muslin and string to make spice bags. A tea caddy will make a good substitute, but you may not want to use it for tea again.

- Jelly bag—the corner of an old pillowcase works well.

- Bowls—a variety of sizes in glass, plastic, or stainless steel.

- Saucepans—stainless steel with a good heavy bottom is best since thin-bottomed pans stick. Aluminum pans will pit from the acid in many foods.

- Colander—such as you would use to drain pasta.

- Diffuser—a variety is available and will be a big help in avoiding stuck and burned mixtures.

- Chopping board—choose one that is easy to keep clean.

- Timer

- Thermometer—a candy thermometer that clips to the side of the pan is best.

- An assortment of crocks, plastic tubs, small plastic buckets, and stone jars as needed.

- Kettles—heavy-bottomed stainless steel is best; aluminum will work but acid mixtures will pit it. Never use cast iron or chipped enamel. A 4- to 6-quart kettle will handle most of these recipes.

- Conventional strainers in various sizes with a fine mesh.

- Large strainer on a stand with a pestle to force food through or a food mill.

- Food grinder—a metal grinder with a variety of blades works well. A food processor will work but it is hard to control and get evenly ground food. Many stand mixers have a grinder attachment that will work well too.

- Blender or food processor—for pureeing mixtures. For a smooth puree, a blender or food processor will work best. If you want more texture, a handheld immersion blender works very well, and for even more texture, a potato masher will often be sufficient.

- Canning jars in a variety of sizes—standard canning jars, also known as Mason jars, come in 8 oz. half pints, 16 oz. pints, and 32 oz. quarts. A few other sizes are occasionally available but these are the most commonly used sizes. You will need these for long-term sealed storage, so buy whatever size you think suits your uses. Pints and quarts also come with standard-size tops and wide-mouth tops. Choose whichever you like. When you purchase your jars, they will come with a removable rim and an inner sealer or lid, which will stay attached to the jar until it is opened for use. The lids should not be reused but the rims can be used many times before being replaced. Replacement lids and rims are readily available at stores selling canning supplies. You may reuse jars and their lids from commercially canned foods that are not standard sizes if they are to be kept in the refrigerator. Kitchen supply stores often sell attrac- tive containers in a variety of size and shapes. They cannot be sealed but will be nice for gifts.

Ingredients

Ingredients are listed at the beginning of each recipe. Be sure to read completely through a recipe to make sure you have everything needed. Remember: your results can be no better than your ingredients, so a few important things to remember are included here.

Produce: Use only the freshest available, store it care- fully, and use as soon as possible. Fruits should be just ripe, not soft, and vegetables crisp and firm.

Vinegar: Do not try to make your own for canning. Vinegar is a preservative and must be 4 to 5 percent acid to be effective. Some of these recipes call for white vinegar and some for cider vinegar.

Each will give a distinctive color and taste but usually can be used interchangeably as personal taste dictates.

Salt: This is also a preservative, so use pure non-iodized

canning or kosher salt. Table salts have iodine and additives to prevent lumping that will result in cloudy syrups. Wherever salt is used in this book, it is understood to be coarse canning or kosher salt.

Spices: Spices will not go bad over time; they will just lose some flavor when kept too long. Whole spices have a longer shelf life than ground. Therefore, buy the size container that you will use up in about a year and store each spice in a cool dark place since sunlight and heat will speed loss of flavor. Whole and ground spices are treated differently when used. Ground spices are added directly to a mixture and will alter the color of the finished product. Whole spices may be added directly or tied in a small fabric or cheesecloth bag and removed just before canning if you do not want them in the finished product. If left in, there will be some addition of flavor. A large tea caddy will work too and is easy to reuse. To some extent, whole and ground spices are interchangeable. A teaspoon of whole spice is equal to about ¼ to ½ teaspoon ground depending on the bulk of the spice. Some experimentation will be necessary when substituting whole for ground (or vice versa). Unless otherwise noted, ground spices are used in these recipes.

Sugar: Acts as both a preserving agent and a thickener. Be sure to use the amounts stated so you get the intended result, especially in the jam and jelly recipes using liquid or powdered pectin. White and brown sugars will give different flavors. Feel free to experiment, but since brown sugars will seem to be a bit sweeter, start with a little less when experimenting. Other sweetening agents such as corn syrup and artificial sweeteners are best left for recipes designed just for their use.

Preserves Information

- Jellies are made from only the clear juice of the fruit.

- Jams contain the juice, fruit pulp and sometimes the skins.

- Marmalades are made from the clear juice of the fruit to which has been added finely chopped pieces of the fruit and its skin or fruit mixtures.

- Butters are the result of cooking the peeled and seeded fruits slowly over low heat.

- Conserves are made by combining fruits with nuts, dried fruits, spices or liqueurs.

- Cheeses are made like butters, but the amount of sugar is increased, and the cooking time lengthened until the mix- ture is stiff.

- Alcohol, in the form of liqueurs, brandy or whiskey also

  - provide a defense against spoilage as well as adding flavor.

CHAPTER 1

CANNING

The Hot Water Bath Method

Some mixtures do not have enough acid or sugar to be safely canned by the open kettle method. For these you will need to use the hot water bath method. This method requires either a special large kettle with a lift-out rack, usually enamel ware, or a smaller kettle with a rack on the bottom that is deep enough so the jars will be covered by at least one inch of water. For this you will also need strong tongs for lifting the finished jars from the water.

1.Fill the kettle about ½ to ⅔ full of hot water, preferably

soft water, cover, and place it over high heat. Bring to a full boil then lower the heat and keep the water at a low boil while filling your jars for processing. Sterilize your jars as explained on page 6.

Also have an extra pan of boiling water ready to fill the canner after the jars are in the water.

2.Prepare the food and fill the jars as the recipe directs:

- **Hot pack**—food is partly cooked before packing into the jars. Then boiling liquid is added to fill the jar to within ½-inch of the top.

- **Cold or raw pack**—uncooked food is packed into jars and then the jars are filled to within ½-inch of the top with boiling liquid.

- Syrups for fruit, hot or cold pack:

- **Very light**—1 cup sugar, 4 cups water

- **Light**—2 cups sugar, 4 cups water

- **Medium**—3 cups sugar, 4 cups water

- **Heavy**—4 to 4¾ cups sugar, 4 cups water

1. Use an absolutely clean wet cloth to wipe off the jar rims.

2. Cover each jar with a sterilized lid and rim. Screw on securely.

3. 3.As each jar is sealed, place it on the wire rack that is suspended over the top of the large water bath kettle. This will start warming the jars and help avoid broken jars. If a conventional kettle is used, place the jars on the rack in the bottom or in a warm oven until all jars are sealed. Boil the water in a separate kettle and pour over the filled jars when all are filled. Jars should not touch each other.

4. When all jars are full, slowly lower the rack into the water. The entire bottom of each jar should hit the boiling water at once. Add boiling water to cover the jars by 1 to 2 inches. Put the lid on the kettle.

5. Return the kettle to a full boil and start timing for the length of time the recipe directs. Adjust the heat to keep the kettle at a boil. If boiling stops, stop timing and resume when the kettle returns to a boil.

6. When the time is done, slowly lift the rack out of the kettle and set it on a folded towel to drain. Wipe the top of each jar. Place the dry jars on a heat-proof surface, out of drafts, to cool. Use tongs to remove the jars from a conventional kettle. Check all jars to be sure the lids are tight.

7. Jars are sealed when the lid is depressed in the center.

8. If a jar does not seal, either refrigerate and use or repeat the processing. Reprocessing is not recom- mended for cucumber pickles and soft fruits.

The Open Kettle Method

Probably the most crucial step in canning is getting the food properly into the jars. Done wrong, your jars will not hold a seal and the food will spoil. Two things are essential for a successfully sealed jar: heat and a clean sterile jar. With- out heat, a vacuum will not form to hold the lid tightly to the jar rim and the lid will not stick to a jar rim with any food on it. By following these basic steps of the open kettle method, you should have no trouble successfully filling and sealing your jars.

1.Prepare the jars:

- Wash the jars carefully and drain.

- Inspect the top rim of each jar and do not use chipped or cracked jars, as they will not seal.

- Sterilize the jars by either boiling, completely submerged, for 10 minutes or by placing the jars in a 225°F oven for at least a half hour. Jars must be at boiling temperature (212°F) or the temperature of the food when they are filled to avoid cracking. If you do not have soft water for boiling, it is better to sterilize your jars in the oven.

1. Prepare the food to be canned according to the recipe.

2. Sterilize the lids inside the rims by boiling them for 10 minutes while the food is cooking. If that time is up before the food is done, lower the heat and return the lids to a boil before using. Soft water works best for this use.

3. Heat the funnel, tongs, cup, or ladle by placing them in the pan with the lids. They need to be hot to avoid a temperature difference, which could crack the hot jars.

4. When food is ready to can, fill and seal one jar at a time unless otherwise directed. Heat is essential so have all equipment ready to use before starting:

- Use tongs to remove two jars from the pan or oven and set them on a heat-proof surface. If the food is not at a boil, let the jars cool a bit before filling to avoid cracking the glass.

- Place the hot funnel on a jar and using a ladle or cup, fill the jar to within a half inch of the top. Use a clean spoon to remove excess food if necessary.

- Put the funnel and cup on the second jar while sealing the first so any drips will go into that jar. A ladle can go back into the pan or on a saucer.

- Use an absolutely clean, damp cloth to wipe the top rim of the filled jar. Any trace of food can cause seal failure. A paper towel will work for this when a small num- ber of jars are to be sealed.

- Use the tongs to remove a lid and rim from the boiling water. Place them on the jar and screw on tightly. Use a hot pad to hold the jar and another to cover the top. A lid tightening device will help here. Your may need to experiment to find the system that works best for you.

- Place the sealed jar on a heat-proof surface to cool but keep it out of drafts. Too rapid cooling can cause jars to crack.

- Before filling the second jar, use the tongs to remove another jar from the kettle or oven and repeat the sealing process.

5. When the jars are completely cool, check them for their seal. Press the center of the lids, which should have been sucked inward at the center and are not flexible.

The rims can now be removed for storage or left on. Label the jars, including the date for easy identification of leftovers when next year's jars are stored. A marking pen will write well on the lids. Store the jars upright in a cool dark place since light and heat can cause darkening over time. Do not freeze the sealed jars. Should any jars not be sealed, store them in the refrigerator and use promptly.

RECIPES

CHAPTER 2

PICKLE RECIPES

PICKLED CAULIFLOWER

Ingredients:

- 1 large head cauliflower

- 3 large yellow or white onions

- ¼ cup coarse salt

- ¾ cup cider or white vinegar

- ¾ cup water

- ¼ to ½ cup sugar, depending on desired sweetness

- 1 teaspoon mustard seed

- ½ teaspoon whole cloves

- ½ teaspoon turmeric

- ½ teaspoon celery seed

- ¼ teaspoon crushed, dry chilies, or more to taste

Directions

1. Break the cauliflower into pieces and wash. Drain well. Peel, quarter, and slice the onions crosswise. Mix the vegetables with the salt and let stand, covered, overnight. Drain well and rinse thoroughly. Let stand in cold water for 30 minutes and drain thoroughly again.

2. Combine the vinegar, water, sugar, mustard seed, cloves, turmeric, celery seed, and chilies and simmer for 10 minutes, covered. Let steep overnight for added flavor.

3. Add the vegetables and boil until tender-crisp, about 5 to 10 minutes. Seal in sterile jars covered with syrup. Yield: approximately 3 pint jars *Note: Extra syrup will be good in salad dressing.

PICKLED FRESH MUSHROOMS

Ingredients:

- 1 lb. button mushrooms

- salt

- ½ cup canola or corn oil

- ¼ to ⅓cupcider vinegar (may bepart lemon juice, if desired)

- ½ cup finely chopped celery

- 4 tablespoons chopped salad olives with pimento

- ¼ to ⅓cup finelychopped red onion, to taste

- 1 tablespoon worcestershire sauce

- 1 tablespoon minced parsley

- 1 clove garlic, minced or crushed

- ½ teaspoon salt

- fresh ground black pepper, to taste

- minced green sweet or hot pepper (optional)

- crushed dry red chilies (optional) Directions

1. Wash and trim the mushrooms. Leave whole if small or cut in half, or quarters if large. Cook for 10 minutes in 1 inch of water and 1 teaspoon salt. Drain well.

2. Gently mix the hot mushrooms with a dressing made by combining the rest of the ingredients. Pour into a quart jar and refrigerate for several days before enjoying. *Note: The jar will not be full to the top. If you wish, more mushrooms may be cooked, but the jar will not hold another whole pound. It will not be necessary to increase the syrup, but if needed, a little more vinegar can be added.

<u>MINTED ONION RINGS</u>

Ingredients:

- medium white onions (see the processing directions for the amount needed)

- 2 cups white or cider vinegar

- 2 tablespoons white sugar

- 2 tablespoons dried mint leaves

- 1 tablespoon coarse salt

- 5 cups white onion rings

- green food coloring

Directions

1. Simmer the vinegar, sugar, mint leaves, and salt together, covered, for 10 minutes. Remove from the heat and let stand while you prepare the onions. There will be more flavor if the syrup steeps overnight.

2. Process enough medium-sized white onions to make 5 cups lightly packed onion rings. Peel the onions and slice them crosswise about ⅜-inch thick. Save the ends for another use and separate the slices into rings. If using large onions, cut in half lengthwise before slicing into half rings. Strain the syrup, if you wish, and add several drops of green food coloring for a brighter appearance.

3. Combine the onion rings and syrup. Heat to boiling, cook 1 minute, and pack in sterile jars. Yield: approximately 2 pints

<u>GOLDEN ONION SLICES</u>

Ingredients:

- 1 tablespoon dry mustard

- 1 tablespoon coarse salt

- 2 teaspoons turmeric, or 1 each of turmeric and curry powder

- 1½ teaspoons black peppercorns, or ½ teaspoon crushed dry red chilies

- 1 teaspoon mustard seed

- ¼ teaspoon cloves

- ¼ teaspoon ginger

- 2 cups cider vinegar

- 2 tablespoons sugar (optional—if you want a slightly sweeter syrup)

- 2 large bermuda onions

Directions

1. Make a syrup by mixing the mustard, salt, turmeric, peppercorns, mustard seed, cloves, ginger, and vinegar (and sugar, if you are using). Simmer together, covered, for 10 min- utes, then set aside to steep while preparing the onions. For added flavor, let steep overnight.

2. Peel the onions, cut in quarters, and slice about ¼-inch thick crosswise. White or Vidalia onions may also be used alone or as a mix. If the onions are smaller, only cut them in half lengthwise before slicing. Place the onions in a large flat kettle. This will help avoid overcooking due to the bottom layers getting hot before the top. If this is not possible, cook the onions in batches since overcooking will give you a soft pickle.

3. Add boiling water to cover and quickly bring just to a boil. Drain in a colander. If the slices are to be sealed, pack them loosely in sterile jars while still hot. Return the syrup to a boil, and pour over the pickles. You may need more vinegar for all the jars, so be sure some of the spices are in each jar and add boiling vinegar as needed.

4. For refrigerator storage, reheat the syrup, add the onions, and let stand at room temperature for several hours before putting into clean jars and covering. Allow to age several days. Yield: approximately 3 pints depending on the size of the onions

PICKLED WHOLE MINI ONIONS

Ingredients:

- 20 oz. bag frozen tiny white peeled onions or 4 cups fresh pickling onions

- ½ cup coarse salt

- water

- 2 cups white or white wine vinegar

- ½ cup white sugar

- 1 tablespoon mixed pickling spices

- ½ teaspoon prepared horseradish, without cream

- ¼ teaspoon crushed chilies

Directions

1. Thaw the frozen onions in cold water and drain well. If using fresh small white pickling onions, immerse them in boiling water for 2 minutes, drain, and chill in cold water. The peel should easily slip off.

2. Make a brine of the salt dissolved in enough water to cover the onions. Add the onions and let stand overnight with a plate on top, weighted down with a water-filled jar. On the next day, drain and rinse the onions well in freshwater.

3. Combine the vinegar, sugar, pickling spices, horseradish, and chilies, and simmer 10 minutes, covered, or let steep overnight for added flavor.

4. Bring the syrup to a boil, remove from the heat, and add the onions. Let stand for 3 minutes to warm the onions. Pack them in sterile jars, reboil the syrup, and pour over the onions, being sure that some of the spices are in each jar. Seal the jars. For refrigerator storage, let the onions cool in

the syrup and pour in to storage jars. Yield: 2 pints *Note: Frozen onions will produce a softer pickle. For crisp pickles, fresh must be used. For added flavor, add to each jar one sliced garlic clove, a small bay leaf, and additional chilies. If any syrup is left over, try it, strained, in salad dressing.

PICKLED BANANA PEPPERS

Ingredients:

- banana peppers (enough to fill 2 pint jars)

- 2 cups cider vinegar

- ½ cup water

- ¼ cup sugar

- 1 teaspoon mixed pickling spices (p. 192)

- 1 teaspoon whole black peppercorns, or a dry chili pepper

- 1 teaspoon mustard seed

- 2 garlic cloves

- 1 teaspoon prepared horseradish, without cream

- 2 small bay leaves

Directions

1. Wash enough banana peppers to fill 2 pint jars, leav- ing a little space for spices. Leave the peppers whole, or if large, cut in half and remove stems and seeds.

2. Combine the vinegar, water, and sugar, and bring to a boil.

3. Fill each pint-sized jar with peppers and add half of the pickling spices, whole black peppercorns, mustard seed, garlic clove (peeled and cut in half), horseradish, and bay leaf.

4. Pour the boiling syrup over the peppers and allow to cool before storing in the refrigerator. Without a hot water processing, which will soften the peppers, it is best to not to seal these pickles for storage. *Note: Other types of peppers, either alone or as a mixture, can also be pickled using this recipe. A slice or two of onion will give a different taste to this recipe as well.

<u>PICKLED PEPPERS</u>

Ingredients:

- peppers of any type (enough to pack into one quart-sized jar)

- bay leaf, broken

- dried chili peppers

- onion, sliced

- peppercorns

- whole cloves

- mustard seed

- coriander seed

- crushed whole dried ginger

- 1½ cups cider vinegar

- ⅓ cup sugar

- 1 teaspoon coarse salt

Directions

1. Wash the peppers, remove stems and cores and cut into large pieces and pack loosely into one sterile quart- sized jar or two pints. Use green or red sweet peppers, yellow banana peppers, hot green peppers, or other types that are available. Select only one type or use a mixture of peppers.

2. Evenly distribute among the peppers, in the desired amounts, the bay leaf, chili peppers, onion, peppercorns, cloves, mustard seed, coriander seed, and dried ginger.

3. Make a syrup by mixing the vinegar, sugar, and salt. Simmer together, covered, for 10 minutes.

4. Cover the peppers with the hot syrup, let cool, and store in the refrigerator for at least 2 weeks before serving. A month is even better.

STUFFED PICKLED PEPPERS

Ingredients:

- 6 small sweet peppers, green or red sweet

- ½ cup coarse salt

- water Seasoning ingredients:

- 3 cups cider vinegar

- 1 cup water

- 3 tablespoons sugar

- 1 teaspoon celery seed

- 1 small cinnamon stick, broken

- 1 teaspoon mustard seed

- 1 teaspoon prepared horseradish, without cream

- 1 teaspoon whole cloves

- 1 teaspoon broken dried ginger root

- 1 teaspoon black peppercorns Filling ingredients:

- 3 cups finely shredded white cabbage

- 1 teaspoon salt

- ¼ cup minced celery

- 1 medium carrot, shredded

- 1 clove garlic, minced

- 2 tablespoons sugar

- 1 tablespoon mustard seed

- 2 teaspoons prepared horseradish, without cream

Directions 1.

1. Wash the peppers, remove and set aside the tops, remove the seeds, but leave the peppers whole. Soak the peppers and their tops overnight in a brine of the salt dis- solved in enough water to cover. Weigh everything down with a plate topped with a water-filled jar.

2. On day 1, also make a spiced vinegar by simmering together vinegar, water, sugar, celery seed, cinnamon, mustard seed, horseradish, ginger root, and peppercorns, for 10 minutes, covered. Set the vinegar aside to steep overnight, covered. The next day, drain and thoroughly rinse the peppers and their tops. Put to dry upside down on

a rack or towel. In a bowl, mix together the shredded cabbage and salt. Let stand for 1 hour, rinse well, and drain very well. Add the celery, carrot, garlic, sugar, mustard seed, and horseradish to the cabbage and mix well. Use to stuff the peppers. Do not pack tightly. Tie the tops on with string.

3. Strain the vinegar, if you wish, and bring to a boil while packing the peppers into two clean, hot quart jars.

4. Slowly pour the vinegar over the peppers, and cover the jars. If you do not strain the vinegar, make sure some of the seasonings are in each jar. This will add flavor. Let cool and store in the refrigerator for several weeks before serving as a cold side dish or heat, but do not boil, in the syrup and serve hot. Yield: approximately 2 quart jars

ZUCCHINI SLICES

- For each quart of finished pickles, you will need the following ingredients:

- 3 zucchinis (about ½ lb.)

- 1 medium white or yellow onion

- 2 tablespoons coarse salt

- 1 cup cider vinegar

- ½ cup white sugar

- 1 teaspoon mustard seeds

- ½ teaspoon cloves

- ½ teaspoon turmeric (optional)

- 1 clove garlic, minced, or ¼ garlic powder (optional)

Directions

1. Slice the zucchini very thinly into enough crosswise slices to measure 1 quart. Thinly slice the onion. Combine the vegetables and mix with salt. Let stand 1 hour and rinse. Drain

2. well and press out the water. The vegetables will have shrunk enough in volume to allow for the bulk of the onion in each quart.

3. Combine the remaining ingredients and simmer for 10 minutes, covered, or let steep while the vegetables are in the brine. Reheat for the next step.

4. Remove syrup from the heat, add the vegetables, and let stand for 1 hour, covered.

5. Pack in 1 hot sterile quart jar or 2 pints, cover with boiling syrup, and store in the refrigerator.

FRESH VEGETABLE PICKLE

This is a nice addition to a snack table. Prepare the vegetables in any amount, using just one type or a mixture, of the following:

- carrots, cut into long, slim sticks

- celery, cut into long, thin sticks

- cauliflower, broken into florets

- small, slender salad onions, leave on some of the green top (if large, they may be cut lengthwise in half or quarter)

- small white pickling onions, peeled

- cucumber, cut to match the other vegetables   Other ingredients for each quart of prepared vegetables:

- 1 cup cider vinegar

- 2 cups water

- 1 cup white sugar

- 1 tablespoon mustard seed

- 1 teaspoon salt, or to taste

- ⅛ teaspoon garlic powder

- ¼ teaspoon onion powder additional ingredients:

- ¼ to ½ teaspoon whole cloves, whole allspice, whole peppercorns, and crushed dried ginger

- several drops hot sauce or crushed red chilies to taste

Directions

1. Measure your prepared vegetables and for every quart, make a brine of 1 quart cold water and 2 Tablespoons pickling or kosher salt. Soak the vegetables in this brine for 2 hours, drain, rinse well and drain again.

2. Pack the veggies into whatever size jar you wish, trimming to fit. Do not overpack. The jars should be clean and hot to avoid breaking when the syrup is added.

3. Combine the vinegar, water, sugar, mustard seed, and salt (add hot sauce or chilies now if using) and simmer, covered, for 10 minutes. The syrup may steep overnight for added flavor. Reheat for the next step.

4. Pour the boiling syrup and spices over the vegetables, being sure some spices are in each jar. Cool to room temperature, and store in the refrigerator. Let age for a week before serving. After enjoying the vegetables, the strained syrup can be used in salad dressing.

<u>**WINTER MIXTURE**</u>

- Prepare 5 quarts of cut vegetables (use only one type if desired, but a mixture is better).

- Choose from:

- cucumber

- celery

- cabbage

- cauliflower

- hot peppers

- red and green sweet peppers

- yellow or white onions

- carrots, sliced or in sticks

- banana peppers

- hot peppers Brine ingredients:

- ¾ cup coarse salt

- 3 quarts water

- Syrup ingredients:

- 3¼ cups vinegar

- 3¼ cups water

- 1 cup sugar

- juice of 1 lemon

- 3 tablespoons mixed pickling spices (p. 192)

- hot pepper sauce or crushed red chilies (optional)

- garlic cloves, minced (optional)

Directions

1. Cut the chosen vegetables into bite-sized pieces trying to get them all about the same size. Make a brine by dissolving the salt in the water. Add the vegetables, cover, and soak overnight, weighted down.

2. Combine the syrup ingredients and simmer, covered, for 15 minutes. Remove from the heat and let steep overnight.

3. On day 2, reheat the syrup and add the vegetables. Let stand for 4 hours, covered.

4. Reheat to almost a boil and quickly pack the hot vegetables in sterile jars. Top with boiling syrup and seal. Be sure to include some of the seasonings in each jar. Yield: approximately 4 quarts *Optional: Add to each jar 1 bay leaf; 1 large garlic clove, sliced; and 1 dry chili, crushed.

SHREDDED SWEET PICKLES

Ingredients:

- 6 cups mixed, coarsely shredded firm vegetables, such as cucumbers, cabbage, onions, and carrots

- ¼ cup coarse salt

- 1 quart water

- syrup ingredients:

- 1½ cups white sugar

- 1½ cups cider vinegar

- 1½ cups water

- 2 tablespoons mustard seed

- ¼ cup pickling spices

Directions

1. Prepare the shredded vegetables. Make a brine of the salt dissolved in the water. Add the vegetables and soak for 4 hours, covered. Drain in a colander and rinse well. Squeeze out as much water as possible.

2. Combine the sugar, vinegar, water, mustard seed, and pickling spices, and simmer together, covered, for 15 minutes. This can be done when the vegetables are set to brine. The extra steeping time will add to the flavor.

3. Reheat the syrup. Add 2 cups of the vegetables to the hot syrup, bring just to a boil, and quickly pack the shreds into a hot sterile pint jar. Top with boiling syrup and seal. Repeat with the rest of the vegetable shreds. Yield: approximately 2 to 2½ pints *Note: Your favorite whole pickling spices may be used instead of the mixed spices.

WATERMELON RIND PICKLES

Ingredients:

- 10 lbs. seedless watermelon

- ½ cup coarse salt

- 2 quarts cold water

- syrup ingredients:

- 3 cups white sugar

- 2 cups cold water

- 2 cups cider vinegar

- 1 large cinnamon stick, broken

- 1 teaspoon whole cloves

- 1 teaspoon whole allspice

- 1 teaspoon cracked dry ginger root

- 1 lemon

Directions

1. Cut the watermelon in half crosswise and then each half into two or three pieces lengthwise. Cut each piece into 1 inch slices crosswise. Remove the red flesh and keep for another use or enjoy as fresh fruit.

2. Lay each slice on its side, cut off just the thin dark green rind with a sharp knife, and cut the light green rind into 1 inch chunks.

3. Make a brine by dissolving the salt in the cold water. Put the chunks in a large pan and pour on the brine. Weigh down the chunks with a plate topped with a water-filled jar so that all chunks are submerged in the brine. Let soak overnight at room temperature.

4. The next day, drain and rinse well under running water in a colander. Redrain and return to the pan. Cover the chunks with fresh cold water and simmer for about 1 hour until tender. Drain well in the colander.

5. Make a syrup of the sugar, cold water, vinegar, cinnamon, cloves, allspice, and ginger root. Simmer for 10 minutes, covered. Add the rind chunks and the lemon, cut in half lengthwise and thinly sliced crosswise. Discard seeds and thick ends.

6. Cook at a simmer, uncovered, for about 1 hour until the chunks appear translucent.

7. Pack the pickles in hot sterile jars, top with syrup, and seal. Make sure some of the spices and lemon are in each jar. Let the pickles age 1 week before enjoying. Yield: 5 to 6 pints *Note: The syrup can be made the night before and let

stand, covered until needed. To make these pickles in summer, choose melon with as thick a rind as possible and follow the recipe. You will want to purchase about 10 pounds of melon. Any extra syrup can be refrigerated to use in another batch of pickles.

SALAD BAR PICKLES

Visit your grocery store's salad bar and select a variety of firm vegetables or purchase them in the produce depart- ment. At home, cut so that the pieces are all about the same size. You will need about 5 cups of cut-up vegetables, such as:

- carrots

- cauliflower

- celery

- cucumber

- onion

- sweet peppers If some heat is wanted, add a jalapeño pepper. A good variety will make a more colorful pickle. Brine ingredients:

- ¼ cup coarse salt

- 1 quart cold water

- syrup ingredients:

- 1 cup water

- 1 cup cider vinegar

- ⅓ to ½ cup sugar

- ½ teaspoon cracked dry ginger

- ½ teaspoon whole cloves

- ½ teaspoon whole allspice

- ½ teaspoon mustard seed

- 1 cinnamon stick, broken

- ¼ teaspoon turmeric

- crushed dry chilies

- dry minced garlic or onion

- celery, dill seed, or dill weed

- ½ teaspoon mustard powder

Directions

1. Mix the vegetables in a nonreactive bowl. Make a brine by dissolving the salt in the cold water and pour over the vegetables. Cover and let stand overnight or about 12 to 14 hours. Drain, rinse well with freshwater, and drain thoroughly again. Taste for saltiness, and if too salty, soak in freshwater for 1 hour or more.

2. At the same time, make the syrup by combining water, vinegar, sugar, spices, cinnamon, turmeric, chilies, garlic or onion, celery or dill seed, and mustard powder in a saucepan. Simmer, covered, for 10 minutes and let steep overnight.

3. Return the syrup to a boil and add the drained vegetables and return to a rolling boil. Pack the pickles in sterile jars, top with boiling syrup being sure that some of the spices are in each jar, and seal. Store in a cool, dry place for several weeks before serving.

4. Yield: 2 pints *Note: You may strain the syrup before using. However, leaving the spices with the pickles adds flavor as they age.

PICKLED CARROTS

Ingredients:

- small carrots

- 1 teaspoon salt

- 1 cup water

- syrup from salad bar pickles recipe

- minced dry garlic, onion powder, mustard seed, hot sauce (optional)

Directions

1. Cut enough small carrots into quarters lengthwise to fill a half-pint jar. Make a brine of the salt and water in a non-reactive bowl, and soak the carrots for 1 hour. Rinse and drain well.

2. Heat the syrup, adding some of the additional seasonings if desired.

3. Add the carrots, bring to a boil, and store in the refrigerator in a half-pint jar or other nonreactive container. Let them age at least 1 week before serving. This is a nice addition to a veggie plate or salad. Yield: 1 half-pint jar

PICKLED MATCHSTICKS

Ingredients:

- ¾ cup cider vinegar

- ¾ cup water

- 1 cinnamon stick, broken

- ½ teaspoon whole cloves

- ½ teaspoon allspice

- ½ teaspoon cracked dry ginger

- 1 long english cucumber

- 1 small to medium yellow or white onion

- 1 tablespoon salt

- ⅓ to½cupsugar or to taste

- 1 teaspoon mustard seed

Directions

1. The night before making the pickles, prepare the syrup. In a saucepan, combine the vinegar, water, cinnamon, and spices. Simmer, covered, for 15 minutes. Leave covered and let stand overnight.

2. The next day, prepare the vegetables. Peel the cucumber, cut lengthwise into quarters, and remove any mature seeds. Cut the quarters crosswise into 3 equal sticks. Cut each stick lengthwise into thin slices and then cut the slices into matchsticks. Peel the onion, cut lengthwise in half, and slice crosswise into thin slices. Separate into half rings.

3. Mix the vegetables in a nonreactive bowl and mix in the salt. Let stand for 1 hour at room temperature. Drain, rinse

well, and press out the water.

4. Strain the syrup and add the sugar and mustard seed. Simmer until the sugar is dissolved, stirring, and bring to a boil. Add the vegetables and return just to a boil. Quickly transfer the vegetables to a hot sterile jar with a slotted spoon. Reboil the syrup and pour over the pickles to fill the jar. Seal and store in a cool dark place for at least 1 week or up to 1 month before serving. The pickles may be stored in the refrigerator unsealed but flavor will develop more slowly that way. Yield: approximately 1½ pints *Note: Flavor variations are easy to create by altering the amount of sugar, adding other spices such as crushed chili peppers, or adding other vegetables such as sweet peppers cut into matchsticks. If you prefer, all the spices may be left in the syrup. In that case, add the mustard seed to the syrup when it is made. A variation on this recipe fol- lows below:

MATCHSTICK DILLS

Syrup ingredients:

- ¾ cup water

- ¾ cup vinegar

- ¼ to ½ teaspoon crushed red chilies

- 1 teaspoon dill seed

- 1 small garlic clove, peeled and smashed

- 2 to 3 tablespoons sugar (added to the drained syrup; dill pickles are not as sweet)

Directions

1. 1.Make the syrup with these ingredients and the pickles as
    in the above recipe.

CHAPTER 3

FRUIT JUICES

<u>APRICOT NECTAR</u>

Calling this fruit's juice "nectar" is a bit of a misnomer. True nectars are produced only by the flowering plant itself. Hummingbirds and insects consume this sweet fluid. What we get from the fruit is juice.

1.   .Use only blemish and bruise free, ripe fruit.

2.   .Wash, pit,and slice fruit.

3.   For every pound, approximately three cups of sliced fruit, add two cups of water.

4.   For a slightly more tart flavor, crack a few pits, remove the inside kernels and add the kernels to the pot. Bring to a simmer until fruit is soft. Remove from heat and press

through a fine sieve.

5.   Return to clean pot.

6.   Add sugar to taste, if desired.

7.   Heat slowly and stir until sugar is dissolved.

8.   If no sugar is being used, heat just to a simmer.

9.   Pour into hot jars, leaving 1/2 inch of head space.

10. .Screw on lids and rings.

11. Process pints and quarts in boiling water bath for 10 minutes.

<u>**BERRY JUICE**</u>

All berries, cherries, and currents may be juiced and canned. The flavor becomes brighter if the fruit is crushed, cooked, strained, and sugar is added, about one cup of sugar to each gallon of juice. Use ripe fruit that is not bruised or damaged.

1.   Crush fruit.

2.   Put a small amount of water in a pot, enough to cover the bottom of the pan to a depth of not more than a half-inch.

3.   Add crushed fruit and over medium-low heat bring to a simmer, stirring frequently.

4.   Continue simmering until fruit is soft.

5.   Strain fruit through a double thickness of cheesecloth set into a colander or sieve.

6.   For a clear juice, do not press on the fruit; let gravity do all the work.

7.   Return juice to pan, add sugar, and return to a simmer, stirring frequently.

8. Pour into jars, leaving 1/2 inch of head room.

9. Screw on lids and rings.

10. Process pints and quarts in boiling water bath for 10 minutes.

TOMATO JUICE

1. Using firm, ripe tomatoes, wash, scald, remove peels and any bruises or damage.

2. Cut into small pieces and place in pot or kettle.

3. .Simmer until soft, stirring occasionally.

4. Put through sieve, being careful to not press seeds through.

5. Put juice in clean pot or kettle and bring to a boil.

6. Pour into hot jars leaving 1/2 inch of head space

7. Wipe rims, screw on lids and rings.

8. Process both pints and quarts in boiling water bath for 15 minutes.

CRANBERRY JUICE

Cranberry juice has long been thought to have curative properties and health benefits. Use by itself, or mix with other fruit juices.

1. Pick over berries; wash well.

2. For each cup of berries, add one cup of water.

3. Bring to boil; maintain boil for 15 minutes.

4. Strain juice through cheesecloth bag. Do not squeeze bag!

5. When all the juice has dripped through, return the pulp to the kettle.

6. Using the original measurement of berries, add 1/2 cup of water for every four cups of berries.

7. Bring to a boil; maintain boil for two minutes.

8. Strain juice through cheesecloth bag.

9. Squeeze fruit to extract all the juice.

10. Combine the two extractions in a clean pot or kettle, measuring juice.

11. For each quart of juice, add one cup of sugar. Stir well.

12. Bring to a boil. Pour into hot jars leaving 1/2 inch of head space.

13. Wipe jar rims, screw on lids and rings.

14. Process both pints and quarts in boiling water bath for 10 minutes.

<u>VEGETABLE JUICE COMBINATION</u>

Use this savory juice as a base for soups or as a refreshing beverage.

1. 1.Using firm, ripe tomatoes, wash, scald, remove peels and any bruises or damage.

2. Cut into quarters, measure and set aside.

3. For each quart of tomatoes, place one chopped, medium-sized onion (white or yellow); 1/2 green bell pepper (seeded & deribbed), chopped; two stalks of celery, leaves set aside and stalks chopped; 1 clove garlic, thinly sliced; 1/4 teaspoon mustard seed, and 1 1/2 teaspoons of salt in a non-reactive container.

4. Mix, cover and set aside for at least four hours, and up to 12 hours.

5. To the tomatoes, add the leaves from the celery stalks, one small bay leaf, and two whole cloves. Mix, cover, and set aside in a non-reactive container.

6. 6.When resting time has been completed, combine the two mixtures and add 1 teaspoon lemon juice.

7. Heat until tomatoes release their juice.

8. Remove from heat and strain juice from vegetables using a food mill to press out about half of the pulp.

9. Discard remaining pulp.

10. Heat reserved juice and pulp in a clean pot or kettle until boiling.

11. Pour into hot jars leaving 1/2 inch of head space

12. Wipe rims, screw on lids and rings.

13. .Process both pints and quarts in boiling water bath for 15 minutes.

GRAPE JUICE

1. Stem and wash ripe grapes.

2. Place in pot or kettle and cover with water.

3. Heat slowly to a simmer; do not boil the grapes.

4. Simmer until grapes are very soft.

5. Strain through a cheesecloth bag.

* Measure juice, and add ½ cup of sugar to each quart of juice.

6. Pour into hot jars, leaving 1/2 inch of head space.

7. Wipe rims, screw on lids and rings.

8. Process both pints and quarts in boiling water bath for 10 minutes. *Stop here to make grape jelly. See recipe under Jellies, Jams, and Marmalades section.

GRAPEFRUIT JUICE

If you are fortunate to live where you can get fresh picked, tree-ripened grapefruit, you can retain that flavor for year-round use by canning grapefruit juice. You must work quickly so the fruit is not exposed to air any more than absolutely necessary.

1. Wash fruit, cut in half and ream the juice from the fruit.

2. Pour juice into sterilized jars, leaving 1/2 inch of head space.

3. To prevent discoloring while stored, add 1/2 teaspoon of ascorbic acid to each quart (1/4 teaspoon per pint). Wipe rims, screw on lids and rings.

4. Process both pints and quarts in boiling water bath for 20 minutes.

CHAPTER 4

MARMALADES

<u>APRICOT LEMON MARMALADE</u>

Ingredients:

- dried apricots

- 1 medium lemon for each cup of chopped dried apricots

- 1 cup of water for each cup of chopped apricots

- Sugar

1. Chop the apricots and measure them. Slice the lemons as in the Apple Marmalade recipe.

2. Add 1 cup of water for each cup of chopped apricots (more may be needed during cooking). Simmer everything for about 45 minutes or until the lemon rind is soft.

3. Measure and add an equal amount of sugar. Follow the basic instructions and seal in sterile jars once complete.

ENGLISH MARMALADE

Ingredients:

- 2 lbs. seville or bitter oranges

- 1 large lemon

- water

- 8 cups sugar

Day One

1. Remove the ends of the oranges and lemon and cut them in quarters lengthwise. Remove the seeds and slice the fruit crosswise as thinly as possible with a sharp knife.

2. Measure everything and put it in a large kettle. Add an equal amount of cold water, stir, cover, and let stand for 24 hours.

Day Two

- Bring the kettle to a boil.

- Remove from the heat, stir well, cover, and let stand

- for 24 hours.

Day Three

1. Bring the jam to a boil. Add the sugar. Stir until the sugar is dissolved and simmer, uncovered, for 2 hours, stirring often. A diffuser under the pan will help avoid sticking.

2. When the peel is transparent and soft, bring to a rapid boil and cook about 30 minutes. Test for setting and continuing cooking until that point is reached.

3. Let stand a few minutes, skim, and seal in sterile jars. Yield: approximately 7 to 8 half-pint jars of marmalade,

depending on the size of the fruit

LIME MARMALADEA ONE-DAY MARMALADE

Ingredients:

- 12 limes

- 7½ cups water

- sugar

- green food coloring

- Remove the green part of the lime rind with a vegetable peeler and shred it thinly with a sharp knife. Process as much rind as you wish. Cut away all the white pith and outer membranes and discard them. Remove the fruit from between the membrane and squeeze any juice from the membranes. Discard the membranes and pith.

- Remove the seeds from the fruit and tie them in a cloth. Chop the fruit or whirl in a blender or food processor.

- Put the fruit, juices, and bag of seeds in a large kettle.

- Add the water and simmer for 1 hour, uncovered. Remove the seed bag and squeeze out the juices.

- Measure the fruit and juices and add an equal amount of sugar and a drop or two of green food coloring. Bring to a boil, stirring, and boil rapidly for about 15 minutes.

- Start testing for jelling, and when thick enough, seal in sterile jars. Yield: approximately 10 half-pint jars of marmalade, depending on the size of the limes

APPLE MARMALADE

Ingredients:

- 1 navel orange

- 1 small lemon

- 6 medium-sized apples (any type of cooking apple

- that will hold its shape will do)

- 2 cups water or complimentary juice

- Sugar

Directions

1. Remove the large ends of the orange and lemon, cut in quarters lengthwise, remove seeds, and thinly slice crosswise. Peel, core, and chop the apples as small as you wish. Add water or a complimentary juice. More liquid may be needed during cooking.

2. Simmer everything for about an hour, stirring often. Cool enough to measure and then add an equal amount of sugar. Follow the basic instructions and seal in sterile jars once complete.

CRANBERRY PINEAPPLE MARMALADE

Ingredients:

- 3 cups cranberry juice cocktail

- 1 standard-sized can crushed pineapple packed in juice, and its juice

- 2 large lemons

- sugar to equal the cooked fruit

1. Remove the large ends of the lemons, cut into quarters lengthwise, remove any seeds, and slice crosswise very thinly. An orange may also be added. Treat the same as the lemons.

2. Simmer for 1 hour in the juice and pineapple. Cool enough to measure and then add an equal amount of sugar. Follow the basic steps and seal in sterile jars once complete.

CHAPTER 5

JELLY

GRAPE JELLY

Ingredients:

- 4 cups bottled concord grape juice, or the same amount made from frozen concentrate mixed with slightly less water than usual

- 7 cups sugar

- ½ bottle or 1 pouch liquid pectin

- Yield: 5 to 6 half-pint jars of jelly

HERB JELLY

This jelly serves as a good accompaniment for meats.

Ingredients:

- 2½ cups water

- 4 tablespoons dried herbs, or 1 cup fresh herb leaves and

- stems, of your choosing

- ¼ cup cider vinegar, wine vinegar, apple juice, or water

- 4½ cups sugar

- yellow or green food coloring (optional)

Directions

1. Begin with an herb infusion: Boil the water and stir in the dried or fresh herbs, lightly packed. Use whatever herbs you prefer or a mixture of several. Cover and let stand for 15 min- utes or as long as overnight for a stronger taste. Strain through a fine sieve and measure 2 cups into a large pan.

2. Add the liquid of your choice (cider vinegar, wine vinegar, apple juice, or water) and the sugar. If you want a brighter color, add a few drops of yellow or green food coloring.

3. Follow the steps for making jam with liquid pectin using a ½ bottle or 1 pouch of pectin. Yield: 5 to 6 half-pint jars of jelly *Note: If using fresh herbs, a leaf may be floated in the center of each jar before sealing. If a sharper taste is desired, add a few drops of hot pepper sauce to the in- fusion before cooking the jelly. A few slices of lemon or orange rind removed with a vegetable peeler can be added when soaking the herbs. A different taste will result from adding a few thin slices of onion when making the infusion. This is a good recipe for experimentation.

WINE JELLY

Ingredients:

- 2 cups wine, whatever type you prefer

- 3 cups sugar

- ½ bottle or 1 pouch liquid pectin

Directions

1. Measure the sugar and wine into a large pan.

2. Cook, stirring, over medium heat until mixture is just below the boiling point.

3. Continue stirring until sugar is dissolved, about 5 minutes, but do not boil.

4. Remove from the heat and at once stir in the pectin.

5. Mix well and skim off the foam.

6. Quickly pour into sterile jars and seal.

7. Yield: approximately

8. 4 half-pint jars of jelly

<u>RASPBERRY JELLY</u>

Ingredients:

- 1 large bag frozen, unsweetened raspberries

- ¾ cup water

- 6 cups sugar

- 1 bottle liquid pectin

Directions

1. Thaw the bag of raspberries completely and crush the berries one layer at a time or whir in a blender or food processor. Scoop the mashed berries into a jelly bag the corner of an old pillowcase works for this. Tie the filled bag tightly and suspend from a cupboard door over a kettle for several hours or overnight. Do not squeeze the bag as this can cloud the juice. When the bag has thoroughly stopped dripping, measure 3 cups into a large pan. Add water if necessary to make this amount.

2. Add water may be part lemon juice and sugar. Pour in 1 whole bottle of liquid pectin.

3. Seal in sterile jars once complete. Yield: approximately 6 half–pint jars of jelly *Note: The fruit left in the bag may be strained to remove the seeds. Sweeten and use as dessert topping or add spices and a little vinegar to use as a relish.

WATERMELON JELLY

Ingredients:

- 3 1-lb. packages of cubed watermelon

- 7½ cups sugar

- juice of 1 lemon

- several drops of red food coloring

- 2 pouches liquid pectin

Directions

1. Cut up, remove seeds, and puree the watermelon in a food processor or blender. Strain overnight through a cloth bag or a large sieve lined with damp paper towels. For jelly, you will want crystal-clear juice.

2. In a large pan, combine 4 cups of watermelon juice, the sugar, lemon juice, and a few drops of red food coloring to give it a rosier color.

3. Follow the basic steps for making liquid pectin jelly.Yield:

approximately 9 half–pint jars of jelly

CRANBERRY JELLY

Ingredients:

- 4 cups cranberries
- ¾ cup sugar for each cup of juice

Directions

1. Cook the cranberries in 3 cups water until very soft. Chopping them first will speed the cooking.

2. Strain the juice through a jelly bag. Measure the juice and add ¾ cup sugar for each cup of juice. Bring to a boil, stirring, and boil to the jelling point.

3. Seal in sterile jars.

WATERMELON SORBET

Ingredients:

- watermelon juice (left over from other recipes)
- ¼ cup of sugar for each cup of juice
- 1 tablespoon fresh lemon juice

Directions

1. In a bowl, for every cup of watermelon juice, add ¼ cup sugar. Add the lemon juice. Stir to dissolve the sugar and let stand for 30 minutes, stirring often and then chill.

2. Place the covered bowl in the freezer and let freeze until almost set. Whip with an electric beater and re- turn to the freezer to freeze completely.

3. Two hours before serving, re-beat and return to the freezer.

Further beating is not necessary for leftovers. *Note: The sorbet can be made in an electric ice cream maker following the directions that come with the

4. machine.

LEMON JELLY

Ingredients:

- 6 lemons

- 7½ cups water

- 2¼ cups sugar for every 2½ cups juice

- yellow food coloring (optional)

Directions

1. Slice the lemons thinly, remove the seeds, and put the fruit into a large pan along with the water. Tie the seeds in a small cloth and add to the pan. The seeds will add extra natural pectin. Bring to a boil and then simmer, covered, for 1½ hours.

2. Strain the juice through a jelly bag. Squeeze the bag of seeds into the jelly bag. Measure the juice and return it to the cleaned kettle.

3. Add 2¼ cups of sugar for every 2½ cups of juice or a scant cup of sugar to each cup of juice. You may add several drops of yellow food coloring for a brighter jelly.

4. Follow the basic method and seal in sterile jars. Yield: will depend on the size of your lemons *Note: A nice addition would be a clean sprig of parsley or a basil leaf suspended in each jar. Be sure to wash and dry the herb first.

<u>TANGERINE JELLY</u>

Ingredients:

- 8 tangerines

- 1 large lemon

- Sugar

Directions

1. Wash the tangerines and lemon, and cut off thin strips of rind with a vegetable peeler. Shred the peel into thin slivers and set aside. Remove all of the white rind and outer membrane. Cut the fruit from the membranes by cutting along the sides of each section. Squeeze juice from the membranes and discard them. Remove seeds from the fruit and tie in a cloth. Chop the fruit by hand or in a blender or food processor.

2. Simmer the fruit, juices, shredded peel, and seeds, covered, for 15 minutes. Strain through a jelly bag overnight.

3. Measure the juice and pour into a kettle. Add an equal amount of sugar and slowly bring to a boil.

4. Cook at a low boil to the setting stage and seal in sterile jars.

TANGERINE JAM

Ingredients:

- leftover pulp from tangerine jelly recipe, previous page
- sugar
- ¼ cup water for every cup fruit
- juice of 1 lemon
- yellow food coloring (optional)

Directions

1. Measure the pulp left from the tangerine jelly in a quart-size measure. Squeeze the seed bag into a kettle and discard the seeds. Add the fruit to the kettle.

2. Add an amount of sugar equal to the measured fruit (scant a little for less sweet jam) and ¼ cup water for every cup fruit. Also add the juice of one lemon and, if desired, a few drops of yellow food coloring for added color.

3. Heat slowly, stirring, and then boil to the setting point as for jam or until desired thickness.

4. Seal in sterile jars.

POMEGRANATE JELLY

Ingredients:

- 6 very ripe pomegranates

- juice of 2 oranges

- finely grated peel and juice of 1 lemon

- sugar

Directions

1. Remove the juice sacks from the pomegranates and mash them, one layer at a time, or whir in a blender or food processor.

2. Add the juice from the oranges, the grated lemon peel, and the lemon juice. Bring the juices to a boil and sim- mer, covered, for 10 minutes.

3. Strain the juices through a jelly bag. Measure and add an equal amount to water. In a kettle, bring to a boil and sim- mer for 20 minutes, uncovered.

4. Let cool enough to measure and add an amount of sugar equal to the reduced juice. Boil to the jelling point and seal in sterile jars.

5. *Note: Add a few drops of red food coloring if jelly appears pale. Cut thin slices of lemon or orange rind with a vegetable parer and float one in each jar of jelly for eye appeal.

CHAPTER 6

JAM RECIPES

APPLE GINGER JAM

Ingredients:

- 3 lbs. tart cooking apples

- 2½ cups water or fresh apple cider

- ¾ cup sugar per cup of fruit

- 2 small lemons, rinds finely grated and juice

- 4 oz. crystallized ginger, finely chopped, or 1 teaspoon powdered ginger

Directions

1. Wash, core roughly, and cut up the apples. Put them in a large kettle and add the water or fresh cider. Cook until the apples are very soft and breaking up. Strain the apples, measure, and return to the kettle.

2. Add ¾ cup sugar per cup of fruit.

3. Add the lemon rind and juice and the ginger.

4. Heat slowly and cook to desired thickness. Seal in sterile jars.

5. Yield: will depend on how thick you want your jam

*Note: Orange juice used in the initial cooking will give this jam a different taste.

APPLE BUTTER

Ingredients:

- 8 lbs. ripe cooking apples, such as mcintosh

- water or apple cider

- ½ cup sugar per cup of strained apples

- 2 teaspoons cinnamon

- ½ teaspoon allspice

- ½ teaspoon cloves

Directions

1. Wash, roughly core, and cut up the apples. Place in a large kettle and add enough water or cider to come about ⅓of the way up theapples. Cook until theapplesare well doneand easily break up. Strain theapples, mea- sure, and return to the kettle.

2. Note: One way to speed up the final cooking of the jam is to cook part of the apples, covered, in the microwave along with a very little water. This will reduce some of the liquid

3. after straining and speed the thickening of the jam.

4. Add about ½ cup sugar per cup of strained apples. You may use brown sugar or some of both brown and white if you prefer. It might be good to scant the sugar and taste before adding it all.

5. Add the cinnamon, allspice, and cloves, adjusting the amounts to your taste.

6. Cook over low heat, stirring often, until desired thickness. Seal in sterile jars.

PUMPKIN PIE BUTTER

Ingredients:

- 1 15-oz. can pumpkin (not pie filling)

- ½ cup brown sugar

- ½ cup white sugar

- 4 tablespoons pure maple syrup

- 1 tablespoon fresh lemon juice

- 1 teaspoon mixed pumpkin pie spice

Directions

1. Mix everything together in a small but deep saucepan. Bring slowly to a boil and then place on a diffuser if possible. Cook very slowly over low heat for ½ hour. Stir often and cover with a lid left slightly ajar to allow steam to escape. This jam will spit badly since it is quite thick to start with.

2. Seal in sterile jars or cool and refrigerate until used.

Yield: approximately 3 half-pint jars of pumpkin butter *Note: If you prefer, replace the commercial mixed pumpkin pie spices with ½ teaspoon cinnamon, ¼ teaspoon cloves, and ¼ teaspoon ginger. The maple syrup may be replaced with either honey or sorghum in the same amount or molasses in half the amount plus 2 tablespoons water. The easiest way to measure the sugars is to pack the brown sugar into the bottom of your cup and then fill it with white sugar. The amounts of all the seasoning can easily be altered to suit your taste, so feel free to experiment. This butter is especially tasty eaten on warm corn muffins.

CRANBERRY PEACH JAM

Ingredients:

- 1 17-oz. can sliced peaches in heavy syrup

- 2 cups fresh cranberries, washed and picked over

- 1 cup golden raisins

- 1 cup water

- 1 teaspoon finely grated orange rind

- 1 teaspoon finely grated lemon rind

- 1 cup sugar

- ½ cup frozen orange juice concentrate, undiluted

Directions

1. In a large pan, combine the cranberries and peaches. Drain the peach juice into the kettle and chop or crush the peaches before adding them.

2. Wash the raisins and squeeze them dry before adding to the mixture.

3. Add the water, grated orange rind, and grated lemon rind. Bring slowly to a boil and simmer for 15 minutes, stirring occasionally

4. Add the sugar and concentrate. Return to a boil and simmer, stirring often, until thick, about 30 to 35 minutes. Seal in sterile jars. Yield: approximately 4 to 5 half-pint jars of jam

***Note:** For a smoother jam, crush with a potato masher after step 3 or use an immersion blender. You may use 2 cups of diced fresh peaches instead of the canned fruit. This will alter the cooking time since there will be less liquid to start with though ripe peaches have quite a lot of juice in them.

FRUIT MEDLEY JAM

Ingredients:

- fresh ripe pears, peeled, cored, and chopped

- fresh peaches, peeled, pit removed, and chopped

- fresh plums, seeds removed and chopped

- sugar

Directions

1. Crush or whirl in a blender or food processor an equal amount of the pears, peaches, and plums. Measure and place in a large pan.

2. Add sugar measured equal to the measured fruit. 3.   Bring slowly to a boil and cook to desired thickness over medium heat. Yield: 7 to 8 half pints to 6 cups of fruit *Note: If fresh peaches are not available, you can use peaches canned in juice, draining before adding. If using

3. canned plums, buy them canned in low-sugar and drain well.

CRANBERRY CONSERVE

Ingredients:

- 4 cups fresh cranberries
- 1½ cups water
- 2½ cups sugar
- 1 cup raisins, golden or dark, washed and squeezed dry
- 1 large cooking apple, such as mcintosh
- finely grated rind and juice of 1 lemon
- finely grated rind and juice of 1 orange
- 1 cup chopped walnuts

Directions

1. Wash and pick over the cranberries. They may be chopped in a blender or food processor if a less chunky jam is desired.

2. Add the water and cook the berries at a simmer until fruit is soft and whole berries pop completely.

3. Add the sugar and raisins. Dried currants may be substituted for raisins. They are smaller so will give a less lumpy jam.

4. Peel, core, and chop the apple and add it along with the grated lemon rind and juice and grated orange rind and juice.

5. Cook at a slow boil until desired thickness.

6. Add the chopped walnuts or other nuts of choice. Reheat to boil and seal in sterile jars. Yield: approximately 8 half-pint jars of jam

***Note:** Chopped dried apricots may be added but add additional sugar if you do so. Fruit juice can also be used in- stead of water to cook the cranberries.

JAM MADE FROM THE PULP LEFT AFTER MAKING JELLY

Ingredients:

- juice and pulp from jelly-making recipes

- 1 cup sugar for each cup of tart fruit pulp (½ to ¾ cup sugar for a sweeter pulp)

- lemon juice, if pulp is extremely thick

Directions

1. After the juice has been removed for jelly-making, strain the pulp to remove any seeds or lumps. Measure the pulp.

2. Add 1 cup sugar for each cup of tart fruit pulp or ½ to ¾ cup sugar for sweeter fruit pulp.

3. Lemon juice or other fruit juice should be added to extremely thick pulp. If it is too thick, it will burn quickly when cooked.

4. Bring the mixture to a slow boil and simmer, stirring, for at least 10 minutes or until of desired thickness. Seal in sterile jars.

* **Note:** Spices and other fruits can be added before cooking for a different taste. When using extremely thick pulp, you may need to add a little water or complimentary fruit juice.

SNOW-TIME CONSERVE

Ingredients:

- 1½ cups cut-up, dried pitted prunes

- 1½ cups chopped dried apricots

- water, apple juice, or orange juice

- 1 seedless orange

- 1 8.75-oz. can crushed pineapple packed in juice

- 5 cups sugar

- ¼ cup lemon juice

Directions

1. In a kettle, almost cover the prunes and apricots with water or fruit juice, and simmer, covered, for 10 minutes, or until the fruit is soft.

2. Remove the orange part of the orange peel with a vegetable peeler. Slice the peel into thin slivers. Add to the kettle while the prunes and apricots are cooking. Remove

3. the orange fruit by cutting on each side of every section. Work over a bowl to catch the juice. Chop the fruit and add juice and fruit to the kettle.

4. Chop the canned pineapple in food processor or blender if a smoother jam is wanted. Add to the kettle along with its juice.

5. Add sugar and lemon juice. Mix everything and boil slowly until of desired thickness. Seal in sterile jars. Yield: approximately 4 to 5 half pints

*Note:** A ¼ cup brandy or orange liqueur will add a dif- ferent taste to this jam. Chopped Maraschino or candied cherries will add more color. For an apricot-only jam, replace the prunes with more apricots. Adding some ginger will give a nice taste to apricot-only jam.

PINEAPPLE JAM

Ingredients:

- 20 oz. can crushed pineapple packed in juice

- 1 tablespoon fresh lemon juice

- ¼ teaspoon ginger (optional)

- yellow food coloring (optional)

- 1½ cups white sugar

Directions

1. Whirl the pineapple in a blender or food processor until fairly smooth. Leave some texture.

2. Add the lemon juice. If you like, add ginger. For a brighter color to your jam, add a drop of yellow food coloring.

3. Simmer, uncovered, for about 45 minutes until quite thick, stirring occasionally. A diffuser will help.

4. Add the sugar and continue simmering for about 30

5. minutes until very thick. Stir often. Test for setting. Seal in sterile jars. Yield: approximately 2½ cups *Note: This is a jam that can easily be personalized by adding other fruits or spices.

PINEAPPLE JAM USING FRESH PINEAPPLE

Ingredients:

- 1 ripe pineapple

- bottled unsweetened pineapple juice

- ¾ cup sugar for each cup pureed fruit

- ¼ teaspoon ginger for each 2 cups fruit (optional)

- yellow food coloring (optional)

Directions

1. Cut off the top of the pineapple and slice in half from top to bottom. Cut each half into at least three sections lengthwise. Lay each piece on its side and slice off the hard core. Cut away the outer rind, being careful to remove all eyes. Next, cut the fruit into small pieces and process in a blender or food processor until fairly smooth. Measure and pour into a large pan.

2. Bring to a boil and simmer, covered, until thick, about 45 to 60 minutes. Add bottled unsweetened pineapple juice as needed and stir occasionally.

3. Add ¾ cup white sugar for each cup of pureed fruit. If you like, add ginger and yellow food coloring to make the jam a brighter color.

4. Return to a simmer and cook uncovered, stirring often, until very thick, about 30 minutes. After cooking for 15 minutes, taste for sweetness and add ¼ cup sugar per cup of fruit if needed. The sweetness of your pineapple will determine the need for extra sugar.

5. Seal in sterile jars. Yield: will be determined by the size of the pineapple

SWEET CHERRY JAM

Ingredients:

- 1½ lbs. frozen, pitted bing cherries

- 1 large mcintosh apple

- 3 tablespoons fresh lemon juice

- 3½ cups white sugar

Directions

1. Thaw the frozen cherries completely. Peel, quarter, core, and chop the apple into small pieces. Chop the mixed fruit in a blender or food processor, in batches, until fairly finely chopped but leave some texture. If necessary, add a little water to make processing easier but do not use more than ½ cup in total. There should be about 4 cups of processed fruit at the end. Pour into a large saucepan.

2. Add the fresh lemon juice. Cook, covered, at a strong simmer until fairly thick, about 1 hour. Add the sugar and continue cooking, uncovered, until jam tests for setting by put- ting a little in the freezer to chill quickly. 3.   Seal in sterile jars. Yield: approximately 5 half-pint jars of jam

Note: After the sugar is added, the jam may be boiled, uncovered, on high heat, but it must be stirred constantly to avoid sticking and burning. *To use fresh Bing cherries, start with about 1¾ lbs. ripe but still firm cherries, Wash, dry, and remove the pits before chopping enough cherries along with the apple to mea- sure 4 cups.

APRICOT JAM

Ingredients:

- 7 oz. bag of dried apricots

- 2 cups water per cup of chopped apricots

- 1 cup white sugar per cup of fruit

- 1 tablespoon fresh lemon juice

Directions

1. Start with dried apricots in whatever quantity you choose. Dice the apricots and measure. One 7 oz. bag will yield about 1 cup chopped apricots.

2. Add 2 cups water per cup of chopped apricots and simmer, covered, about 2 hours until the fruit is very soft and the water is well reduced. Mash with a potato masher or whirl in a blender or food processor until the desired smoothness.

3. Measure the fruit, and for each cup, add 1 cup sugar. Add the lemon juice.

4. Simmer, uncovered, at least 10 minutes or until desired thickness, stirring often. A diffuser under the pan will help avoid sticking. Seal in sterile jars or store in the refrigerator. Yield: approximately 2 cups jam per cup of chopped apricots *Note: You may prefer to add the water a cup at a time as the cooking progresses. Interesting additions might be ginger, chopped apples, or other fruits.

APRICOT ORANGE JAM

Ingredients:

- 7 oz. bag dried apricots

- 2 small navel oranges

- 2 cups water

- 1 cup sugar for each cup cooked fruit

Directions

1. Dice the apricots. Quarter the oranges lengthwise, trimming away the thick rind at each end, and slice thinly. Combine the fruit with water in a heavy-bottomed saucepan.

2. Simmer, covered, for about 2 hours until everything is very soft and liquid is well reduced. If there is too much liquid when the fruit is soft, raise the heat and boil, stirring constantly, until reduced. For a smoother jam, mash with a potato masher but leave some texture.

3. Measure the fruit. Return to the pan and add the sugar.

4. Continue simmering until the jam is quite thick and tests for setting. Seal in sterile jars. Yield: 5 half-pint jars of jam *Optional: Add ½ teaspoon powdered ginger or more to taste. Puree the apricots and add to the oranges when measuring for sugar. This will leave the orange slices whole, more like marmalade. Adding a chopped cooking apple such as McIntosh will give a milder jam.

PEACH AND ORANGE JAM

Ingredients:

- 1½ lbs. frozen sliced peaches

- 1 navel orange

- ¼ cup water

- 1 tablespoon fresh lemon juice

- 2 cups sugar

- ¼ teaspoon ginger (optional)

Directions

1. Thaw the peaches. Shred the orange part of the rind using the next to the largest holes on your grater and put the shreds into a saucepan. Remove the rest of the rind and the outer membrane. Cut between the dividing membranes and remove the fruit sections. Work over a bowl to catch any drips and include any juice squeezed from the membranes.

2. Whirl all the fruit in a blender or food processor in batches until well chopped but not completely pureed. There will be about 3 cups of processed fruit. Place in a saucepan or kettle.

3. Use the water to rinse out the machine and add it along with the lemon juice to the fruit. Cook, uncovered, at a simmer for about 30 minutes until the fruit bits are very soft and the volume is somewhat reduced. Stir often.

4. Add the sugar and, if you desire, the ginger. You can also add chopped Maraschino cherries for extra color.

5. Return to a simmer, stirring, and taste for sweetness. If desired, add up to ½ cup additional sugar. Continue cooking for about 20 minutes and start to test for setting.

6. Seal in sterile jars. Yield: approximately 4 half-pint jars of jam

*Note: Fresh peaches may be used. Peel, slice, and process enough to measure 3 cups when added to the processed orange.

APRICOT JAM FROM DRIED APRICOTS

Ingredients:

- ½ lb. dried apricots

- ¼ cup lemon juice

- 7 cups sugar Directions

Directions

1. Wash and drain the dried apricots, and place in a saucepan with 3¾ cups water. Leave to soak at room temperature for at least 4 hours, or overnight.

2. .When soaking is complete, simmer in the pan, covered, for about 30 minutes to soften and break up the fruit.

3. Measure 3¾ cups of the fruit and place in a large pan.

4. Add water if there is not enough fruit. If large pieces of fruit are not wanted, cut up the apricots before cooking or mash when soft.

5. Add the lemon juice and sugar. For a taste variety, use orange juice in place of part of the water for cooking or add some finely grated lemon or orange rind.

6. Follow the basic jam-making steps and add 1 whole bottle of pectin or 2 pouches. Yield: approximately 8 half-pint jars of jam

STRAWBERRY PINEAPPLE JAM

Ingredients:

- 10 oz. box of frozen, whole strawberries, or 1 cup crushed fresh strawberries

- 20 oz. can crushed pineapple packed in juice

- ¼ cup water

- 3½ cups sugar

- 1 bottle or 2 pouches liquid pectin Directions

Directions

1. Thaw the frozen strawberries. Thoroughly crush the berries in their juice. Measure 1 cup, including the juice, and put into a large pan or use the fresh berries. Save any extra for another use.

2. Drain the pineapple well and use the juice for something else if desired. Add the pineapple to the berries.

3. .Add the water and sugar to the mixture.

4. Follow the basic steps in jam-making and seal in sterile jars. Yield: approximately 5½ half-pint jars of jam

BANANA BUTTER

Ingredients:

- 8 to 10 ripe bananas (should be soft but not black)

- 6 cups sugar

- juice of 1 large lemon

- 1 bottle or 2 pouches liquid pectin

Directions

1. Crush the bananas to a pulp with a potato masher or use a food processor or blender being careful not to over-process and incorporate excess air. Crush part of the bananas at a time and measure as you go along. A quart glass measure works well for this. You will need 1 and ½ lbs. of processed fruit, and this is one place where weighing helps (a pound is around a pint measure). Put the crushed fruit in a large pan.

2. Add the sugar and lemon juice.

3. Heat slowly, stirring constantly, until boiling and the sugar has dissolved. Cook at a rolling boil for 1 minute.

4. Add the pectin and follow the basic steps in jam-making and seal in sterile jars. Yield: about 5 half-pint jars of jam. However, this will vary by the ripeness of the fruit. *Optional: Add grated citrus fruit rind to taste.

FROZEN UNCOOKED BLUEBERRY JAM

Ingredients:

- 3 12-oz. packages of frozen blueberries, or an equal amount of fresh berries

- 5 cups sugar

- ¼ teaspoon cinnamon

- 1 bottle or 2 pouches liquid pectin

- 2 tablespoons lemon juice

Directions

1. Thaw the blueberries. Crush the berries with a potato masher, one layer at a time, measuring as you go (should yield about 4½ cups of crushed fruit). Put the fruit into a bowl or large pan. Fresh berries will work too, but be sure they are ripe.

2. Add the sugar and cinnamon. Mix thoroughly and let stand for 30 minutes.

3. In a small bowl, combine the liquid pectin and lemon juice. Stir the pectin into the fruit and stir for 3 to 5 minutes to dis- solve the sugar.

4. Ladle into clean freezer containers and cover tightly.

5. Let sit at room temperature about 24 hours or until jel- lied.

6. Store in the freezer until ready to use. The jam will keep in a refrigerator for 2 to 3 weeks after thawing.

GINGER PEAR JAM

Ingredients:

- 3 lbs. pears, whatever type is readily available

- 1–2 teaspoons powdered ginger (adjust to taste)

- 7½ cups sugar

- ¼ cup lemon juice

- 1 bottle or 2 pouches liquid pectin

Directions

1. Peel, remove cores, and grind or chop the pears very finely. A food processor may be used but leave a little texture. Measure 4 cups of fruit and put into a large pan.

2. Add the powdered ginger, sugar, and lemon juice. Mix well and bring to a full rolling boil for 1 minute.

3. Add the liquid pectin. Follow the basic steps for jam-making and seal in sterile jars. Yield: 8 to 10 half-pint jars of jam *Optional: Vary the spices with cinnamon, cloves, and allspice to taste. For a more spicy taste, substitute vinegar for the lemon juice.

CHAPTER 7

MINCE MEAT RECIPES

MEATLESS MINCEMEAT

Ingredients:

- 3 firm, tart cooking apples

- ½ lb. beef suet

- 2 cups raisins

- 1 cup mixed candied fruit

- 1 large navel orange

- juices from ground fruit

- juice, cider, or apple brandy (if needed)

- 1 cup brown sugar

- 1 cup currants

- ½ teaspoon allspice

- ½ teaspoon cloves

- ½ teaspoon cinnamon

- ½ teaspoon salt

Directions

1. Peel the apples, core, and chop coarsely. Chop the suet. Wash and squeeze dry the raisins. Grate the orange rind and remove the fruit from the pith and membranes. Mix the ingredients and grind, collecting the juices. Place the ground mixture in a large saucepan.

2. Measure the reserved juices and use another juice or brandy to make the liquid total 1 cup. Mix into the fruit.

3. Add the sugar, currants (wash and squeeze dry), spices, and salt. Mix well and cook at a simmer for 45 minutes to 1 hour, adding juice if too dry. Using a diffuser over the burned will help avoid sticking. Store in the refrigerator. Yield: 2 to 3 pints

GREEN TOMATO MINCEMEAT

Ingredients:

- 4 cups finely chopped green tomatoes,
- 2 cups peeled, cored, and chopped tart cooking
- apples
- 1 orange
- 2 cups raisins
- ½ cup ground or chopped finely candied fruit peels,
- 2 cups brown sugar
- ½ teaspoon cloves
- ½ teaspoon allspice
- ½ teaspoon ginger
- ½ teaspoon salt
- apple or orange juice, as needed

Directions

1. Grate the orange rind and remove the white pith. Cut the fruit from between the membranes, and chop. Squeeze the juice from the membranes. Wash, squeeze dry, and chop the raisins.

2. Combine all ingredients in a heavy-bottomed pan and simmer for about 1 hour, adding fruit juices, such as apple or orange, as needed to keep from sticking. Store as above. Yield: 2 to 3 pints

MOM'S MINCEMEAT

Ingredients:

- 2 cups lean beef (stew meat works best)
- 4 cups peeled, cored, and chopped tart apples
- 2 cups raisins
- 2 cups currants
- 1 cup chopped citron
- 1 cup chopped beef suet
- 2 cups sugar
- 1 cup cider or fruit juice
- 1 cup beef stock (from cooking meat)
- 2 teaspoons salt
- 1 teaspoon nutmeg
- 1 teaspoon cloves
- 1 teaspoon cinnamon

1. Remove as much fat as possible from the meat and simmer in water until well done. Drain and save the broth. Mix together with the apples, raisins and currants (washed and squeezed dry), citron, and beef suet. Grind the mixture and transfer to a heavy bottomed kettle. Add sugar, cider/fruit juice, beef stock, salt, and spices. Mix well and simmer slowly for 1 hour. When the cooking time is half over, taste the mincemeat and adjust the seasonings to your taste. If more liquid is needed, add juice, brandy, or rum a little at a time. Store as above. Yield: approximately 6 pints

FRUITED MINCEMEAT

Ingredients:

- 1 cup chopped beef suet
- 1 cup chopped dried apricots
- 1 cup chopped dried peaches
- 1 cup peeled chopped carrots
- 1 cup raisins
- ½ cup diced citron
- 4 large, peeled and chopped tart apples
- 3 navel oranges
- 2 cups sugar, brown or white
- 1 cup cider or fruit juice
- 1 teaspoon cinnamon
- ½ teaspoon cloves
- ½ teaspoon allspice
- ½ teaspoon mace
- ½ teaspoon ginger

Directions

1. Mix and grind together the suet, apricots, peaches, carrots, raisins, citron, apples, and oranges (grate the rind, remove the fruit from the pith and membranes, squeeze the juice out, and chop the fruit). Transfer to a large heavy-bottomed pan and add the orange juice and rind, and the rest of the ingredients.

2. Mix well and simmer until well blended and fruits are tender, about 1 to 1½ hours. Add additional juice, a little at a time, if mixture becomes too dry. Store as above. Yield: 5 to 6 pints

<u>WILD GAME MINCEMEAT</u>

Ingredients:

- 3 cups cooked and chopped lean meat (such as
- moose, deer, or elk)
- 1 cup chopped beef suet
- 3 tart apples
- 1 cup raisins
- 1 cup currants
- ½ cup diced citron
- 1 cup diced mixed candied fruit peel
- 2 cups apples juice
- 1½ cups brown sugar
- 1 tablespoon cinnamon

- 1 teaspoon ginger

- ½ teaspoon cloves

- ½ teaspoon allspice

- ½ teaspoon mace

- ½ teaspoon salt

Directions

1. Peel and core the apples. Wash and squeeze dry the raisins and currants. Mix and grind these together with the meat, suet, and candied fruit peel. Transfer to a heavy- bottomed pan.

2. Add the apple juice, sugar, cinnamon, ginger, spices, and salt. Mix well and simmer until thickened, adding juice a little at a time, if needed. At the end, you may wish to add brandy or rum for extra flavor. Store as above. Yield: approximately 4 cups of mincemeat depending on how long it is cooked *Note: Candied fruit peels are most often available around Christmastime when they are marketed for making fruitcake, but larger stores may have them all year.

CHAPTER 8

MISCELLANEOUS: SWEET FRUIT SAUCES, SYRUPS, AND RELISHES

<u>APPLESAUCE</u>

Ingredients:

- red cooking apples, such as mcintosh in whatever

- amount you wish

- water

- sugar

- cinnamon (optional)

- red food coloring (optional)

Directions

1. Wash, trim, cut up, and roughly core the apples. You do not need to remove the entire core since it will be removed when the sauce is strained. Put them into a kettle and add about ¾ cup water for each quart of cut-up apples or water about one-third of the way up the filled kettle. Bring to a boil and cook at a low boil until the apples are very soft stirring occasionally. Strain the apples, mea- sure, and return to the kettle.

2. Add about ½ to ⅝ cup of sugar per quart of strained apples. If you like, you may also add 1 teaspoon of cin- namon per 4 quarts of the strained apples, or to taste. Adding a few drops of red food coloring will give the sauce a pleasantly rosy color.

3. Return slowly to a boil, stirring, and simmer for 10 minutes. Cook longer if too watery. Seal in sterile jars or freezer containers. A peck of apples, 8 quarts, will yield about 4 to 5 quarts of sauce and a bushel 20 to 25 quarts depending on how thick you want your sauce.

CINNAMON APPLES

Ingredients:

- 4 large firm apples (choose a type that will hold its

- shape when cooked)

- ½ cup water

- ½ cup sugar

- ½ cup little red cinnamon candies (red hots)

Directions

1. Wash, peel, and cut the apples into fairly thick wedges, about 6 per apple. Alternatively, cut crosswise into thick rounds and remove the cores.

2. In a straight-sided fry pan or large saucepan, make a syrup of the water, sugar, and cinnamon candies.

3. Simmer until the sugar and candies are dissolved, stirring constantly.

4. Add the apples, one layer at a time, and simmer until the apples are somewhat transparent but still holding shape. Cool on a plate and refrigerate. Yield: approximately 24 apple slices *Note: These slices are especially pretty served as a holiday salad when arranged in a flower shape on a lettuce leaf with a ball of cream cheese that has been rolled in chopped nuts in the center. The syrup left after cooking is a tasty addition to applesauce or served warm over desserts.

"LUMPY" APPLESAUCE

Ingredients:

- apples (choose cooking apples such as mcintosh in

- any amount you wish)

- water

- sugar

- ⅛ to ¼ teaspoon cinnamon (optional)

- red food coloring (optional)

Directions

1. This applesauce does not get strained, so it will need a few extra preparation steps. Choose whatever type of apples you prefer, but ones that fall apart when cooked are preferable. To prepare the apples, peel, quarter, core, slice, and chop roughly. Place the apple chunks in a pan and keep underwater until all apples are prepared. This will help prevent browning.

2. When all apples are chopped, drain off the water until it only comes up the side of the pan about ⅓ the depth of theapples. Cook slowly until theapplesaresoft. If thechunks do not fall apart when theyare very soft, mash with a potato masher or whir in a blender or food processor but leave small pieces for texture.

3. Measure the sauce and add ½ to ⅝ cup sugar per quart, taste before adding more. If you choose, you may add cinnamon and red food coloring for a rosy color.

4. Return the sauce to a simmer and cook, stirring often for 10 minutes and seal in sterile jars, freezer containers, or refrigerate once cool. Yield: will be about the same as for strained applesauce

RUM RAISIN SAUCE

Ingredients:

- 1 cup sugar

- ⅓cup water

- 2 cups dark raisins or currants

- 1 small orange

- ½ cup water

- ⅓ to½cup rum, preferably dark rum

Directions

1. Combine the sugar and water. Bring to a boil, stirring.

2. Wash the raisins or currants, picking over for any stems, and squeeze dry. Coarsely grate the orange rind and add along with the additional water to the mixture.

3. Simmer slowly for 15 minutes or more, covered, until quite thick, then cool until just warm and add the rum.

4. Store in a covered container at room temperature for several days. Use as a topping for ice cream, pudding, or cake and other desserts. Yield: depends on how thick you make the sauce but it will be between 1½ to 2 cups *Note: Variations can be made by using other dried, chopped fruits alone or with the raisins. Fruit-flavored liqueurs, such as peach brandy or orange liqueurs, can be used in- stead of the rum. The juice of the orange may be used in- stead of all or part of the water.

APPLE CATSUP

Ingredients:

- 4 lbs. firm apples, such as mcintosh

- 2 cups cider vinegar

- 3 cups sugar

- 1 teaspoon whole cloves

- ½ teaspoon whole allspice

- ½ teaspoon peppercorns

- 1 cinnamon stick, broken

- 2 teaspoons mustard seed

Directions

1. Make the apples into an unsweetened applesauce using as little water as possible.

2. Meanwhile, make a syrup by combining the remaining ingredients. If you prefer, the spices may be contained in a spice bag or tea caddy and removed when the sauce is done. Alternatively, you may substitute ground spices for the whole:

   - ¼ teaspoon cloves

   - ⅛ teaspoon allspice

   - ⅛ teaspoon black pepper

   - ¼ teaspoon dry mustard

   - Your sauce will be darker and some experimentation may be needed.

3. Bring the syrup to a boil and simmer, tightly covered, for 30 minutes. For more flavor, make it the day ahead, sim- mer, and let stand overnight. Strain to remove the whole spices if left loose, and add the cooked strained apples.

4. Return to a simmer and cook for 20 to 30 minutes or until very thick. Stir often. A diffuser on the burner will be a big help.

5. Seal in sterile jars. Yield: will depend on the size of the apples and how thick the catsup—approximately 2 to 3 pints

<u>LEMON CATSUP</u>

This syrup is quite tart and spicy. Try it on seafood or chicken.

Ingredients:

- 12 medium, or 10 large, lemons

- 1 cup sugar

- 1 tablespoon grated fresh horseradish (or use bottled pure horseradish without cream)

- 1 tablespoon powdered mustard

- 1 teaspoon turmeric

- ½ teaspoon cloves

- ½ teaspoon allspice

- ½ teaspoon ground white pepper

- 1 small onion, minced

- a dash of cayenne pepper, or more to taste

Directions

1. Coarsely grate the rind from each lemon and juice all of them. Add sugar, horseradish, powdered mustard, turmeric, cloves, allspice, white pepper, finely minced onion, and cayenne pepper. Mix well and let stand, covered, overnight in a nonreactive container such as plastic, glass, or stainless steel.

2. The next day, bring to a boil and cook slowly, uncovered, for 30 minutes. Return to a tightly covered container and let stand for two weeks in a cool dark place, stirring daily.

3. Strain through a jelly bag, bring to a boil, and seal in sterile jars or refrigerate. Yield: approximately 2 pints *Note: This sauce is quite thin, so serving from a small bottle or with a spoon is a good idea. It would freeze well, perhaps as ice cubes, for using a little at a time.

APRICOT SAUCE

Ingredients:

- 11 oz. dried apricots

- 1 cup dark corn syrup

- 1 cup light corn syrup or basic sugar syrup (see below)

- ½ cup water

- juice of 1 lemon or orange

Directions

1. Cook the dried apricots slowly, covered, in enough water to almost cover, until very tender and water is almost gone. Puree in a blender or food processor.

2. Transfer to a pan and add the dark corn syrup, light corn syrup (or basic sugar syrup), water, and juice.

3. Bring to a boil and simmer 10 to 15 minutes or until sauce as thick as you wish. Seal in sterile jars or refrigerate. This makes an excellent dessert or pancake topping.

Yield: approximately 2 to 3 pints depending on thickness *Note: The same sauce can be made using 2 standard cans of apricots packed in as low sugar syrup as possible. Skip the first cooking, drain the apricots, and puree keeping the juices. Adjust the amount of sweetening added and mix in as much of the apricot juice as needed to make the tex- ture you prefer. You will need to simmer the syrup for 10 min- utes if it is to be sealed in sterile jars.

BASIC SUGAR SYRUP TO USE IN FRUIT SYRUPS

Ingredients:

- 2¼ cups sugar

- 2½ cups water

1. Dissolve the sugar in the water over low heat. Bring to a boil and cook to 220°F. Skim off any foam and store in the refrigerator tightly covered. Use within a week.

CRANBERRY SYRUP

Ingredients:

- 4 cups fresh cranberries

- 2½ cups basic syrup

- juice of 1 lemon

- ⅓cup red port wine (optional)

1. Wash and pick over the cranberries. You may chop if desired. Add the basic syrup and lemon juice. 2. Cook at a slow boil for 10 minutes or until the cranber- ries are very soft. Cool and strain. For a clearer syrup, use a jelly bag. Add red port wine if desired. For additional flavor, let the cook fruit stand for several days before straining. Store in the refrigerator or seal in sterile jars.

Yield: will depend on how you strain the sauce and on how long it is cooked but there should be between 3 and 4 cups of syrup *Note: All these fruit syrups will make attractive gifts in assorted small bottles.

POMEGRANATE SYRUP

Ingredients:

- 2 pomegranates

- juice of 1 lemon

- 2 cups basic syrup

Directions

1. Remove the seed sacks from the pomegranates and crush or whir in a blender or food processor. Strain the juice overnight using a fine mesh sieve or jelly bag.

2. Add the lemon juice and the basic syrup. Mix well, taste, and adjust the sweetness. For a sweeter sauce, add more of the basic syrup. Additional lemon juice will decrease the sweetness. Yield: determined by how sweet or thick you make the syrup; uncooked syrup will give you around 3 cups *Note: For thicker syrup, simmer the juices until quite thick and then add the syrup. Seal in sterile jars or refrigerate. For a refreshing drink, mix the syrup with soda water or a lemon/ lime soda. You might prefer a less sweet syrup for use with a sweetened soda.

CINNAMON SYRUP

Ingredients:

- 4 cups fresh apple juice (if using bottled, make sure it has as little sugar as possible)

- 1 cup basic syrup

- ½ cup red cinnamon candies (red hots)

- 1 cinnamon stick, broken

- additional basic syrup or lemon juice for adjusting sweetness

Directions

1. Mix all ingredients except the additional syrup or lemon juice and simmer, uncovered, until fairly thick and syrupy.

2. Taste and adjust sweetness by adding additional syrup or a bit of lemon juice. Remove the cinnamon stick bits and seal in sterile jars or refrigerate for storage.

Yield: determined by how thick the syrup becomes; there will be around 3 to 4 cups of cinnamon syrup *Note: For additional flavor, let the syrup stand for several days before straining.

GINGER SYRUP

Ingredients:

- fresh ginger root

- 1 lemon

- 2½ cups basic syrup

Directions

1. Peel and finely chop or grate enough ginger root to measure 3 tablespoons. Coarsely grate the lemon rind and juice the lemon. Combine these with the basic syrup.

2. Simmer for 10 minutes, uncovered, and let stand overnight or longer. Strain and seal in sterile jars or refrigerate. Yield: approximately 2½ cups of ginger syrup *Note: To seal these syrups, first return them slowly to a boil and then seal in hot jars. Pour into clean jars and cover to store in the refrigerator or pour into freezer containers and freeze.

GOLDEN RELISH

Ingredients:

- 6 long, slim ripe cucumbers

- 5 medium onions, white or yellow

- ¼ cup coarse salt

- water

- 2 cups cider vinegar

- 1 cup sugar

- 2 teaspoons turmeric

- 1 teaspoon mustard seed

- ½ teaspoon dry mustard

- ¼ teaspoon cinnamon

- ¼ teaspoon cloves

- ¼ teaspoon allspice

Directions

1. Peel and finely chop or grind the vegetables. Add the salt and water to cover. Let for stand 2 hours, rinse and drain well. Press out as much water as possible.

2. In a separate pan, combine the vinegar, sugar, tur- meric, mustard seed, dry mustard, and spices and simmer, covered, for 10 minutes. Let stand while the vegetables are in the brine.

3. Add vegetables to the syrup and simmer until vegetables are tender and yellow in color. Seal in sterile jars. Yield: approximately 2 to 3 pints *Note: Collect the juices while grinding the vegetables for the relish. Freeze the juice in ice cube trays, store in plastic bags in the freezer, and use in soups and stews for added flavor.

UNCOOKED RELISH

Ingredients:

- ¼ head of cabbage

- 1 green sweet pepper

- 1 medium yellow onion

- 2 slender cucumbers, peeled and deseeded

- ¼ cup coarse salt

- 1 large apple, such as granny smith or golden delicious,

- peeled and cored

- syrup ingredients:

- 2 cups cider vinegar

- 1 cup white sugar

- 2 teaspoons mustard seed

- ¼ teaspoon celery seed

- ½ teaspoon cloves

- ½ teaspoon allspice

Directions

1. Grind together the vegetables, add the salt, and let it drain overnight in a cloth bag or strainer.

2. Combine the syrup ingredients in a pan large enough to hold the ground vegetables. Simmer together for 15 minutes, covered. This can be done the night before and left to steep overnight for more flavor.

3. Grind the apple and add to the syrup along with any juice. Rinse and drain the vegetables well and add to the syrup. Bring just to a boil and let cool in the pan. Store in the refrigerator in clean jars for at least 1 week before using. Yield: depending on the size of your vegetables, you will have between 3 and 4 pints *Note: To make this a cooked relish, cook as in the above recipe and seal in sterile jars. For additional color, replace some of the green pepper with red sweet pepper. If heat is desired, grind some hot pepper with the other vegetables.

BROCCOLI SLAW RELISH

Ingredients:

- 12 oz. bag broccoli slaw

- 1 medium onion

- 1 red sweet pepper, sliced (optional)

- 1 or more small hot peppers (optional)

- 2 tablespoons coarse salt

- syrup ingredients:

- ¾ cup water

- ½ cup vinegar

- ½ cup sugar, brown or white

- 2 teaspoons mustard seed

- ¼ teaspoon cloves

- ¼ teaspoon allspice

- ½ teaspoon turmeric (optional—will give the relish a golden color)

- garlic powder, cayenne pepper, celery seed, and minced parsley (optional)

Directions

1. For easier grinding, first chop the slaw to cut up the long shreds. Grind the slaw and onion and, if you want additional color, grind several slices of red sweet pepper. For heat, grind up the hot pepper. You should have 3 to 4 cups after grinding the vegetables.

2. Mix in the salt. Let stand for 1 hour, then rinse well in batches using a fine mesh strainer. Taste for saltiness, and if too salty, soak in cold water for 30 minutes and rinse again. Press out as much water as possible.

3. Combine the syrup ingredients and simmer for 10 minutes, covered. Let stand while the vegetables are salting.

4. Add the vegetables to the syrup and cook at a sim- mer, uncovered, until the vegetables are tender and liquid

<u>WINTER RELISH</u>

Ingredients:

- 3 long, slender cucumbers

- 3 medium to large yellow or white onions

- 1 small head cabbage, or half a large head

- 3 green peppers, or 1 red and 2 green

- 2 large garlic cloves, or to taste

- 3 large carrots

- ¼ cup coarse salt

- syrup ingredients:

- 1½ cups cider vinegar

- ½ cup brown sugar

- ½ cup white sugar

- 1 tablespoon mustard seed

- ½ teaspoon cloves

- ½ teaspoon allspice

- ½ teaspoon turmeric (optional—will give relish a golden color)

- ¼ to ½ teaspoon cayenne pepper (optional)

Directions

1. Peel, quarter, and seed the cucumbers. Peel the onions. Trim the cabbage and wash and remove the seeds from the peppers. Peel the garlic. Scrape or peel the carrots. Cut all vegetables into small chunks and mix together. You will have about 5½ quarts of cut vegetables. Grind them and drain well. Collect the juice and save it to flavor soups or stews.

2. Mix the ground vegetables with the salt, add water to cover, and soak for 1 hour. Drain well by batches in a strainer, pressing water out gently. Put in a kettle.

3. Add the syrup ingredients, mix well, and cook at a sim- mer about 30 minutes, or until vegetables are tender and the relish is not too runny. Add water or vegetable juice if it becomes too dry. Yield: approximately 4 pints

ANOTHER GREEN TOMATO RELISH

Ingredients:

- 1 rounded qt. roughly chopped green tomatoes

- ¼ cup coarse salt

- ½ small head of cabbage

- 1 green pepper

- 1 small red sweet pepper

- 3 medium onions

- garlic cloves (optional)

- hot peppers (optional)

- Syrup ingredients:

- 2 cups cider vinegar

- ½ to 1 cup brown or white sugar

- 1 tablespoon mustard seed

- 1 teaspoon cloves

- 1 teaspoon allspice

- ½ teaspoon turmeric, cayenne pepper, garlic powder, and celery seed (optional)

1. **Day 1:**

Prepare the green tomatoes. Wash, cut up, grind, discarding the juice, and measure. There should be about 2 cups ground tomatoes. Add the salt, mix, and drain overnight in a strainer, colander lined with paper towels, or in a cloth bag.

2. **Day 2:**

Grind together the cabbage, green pepper, red sweet pepper, and onion (add garlic cloves and hot pepper here, if using). Drain and set aside excess juices and measure the vegetables. There should be about 4½ to 5 cups. 3.

In a kettle, combine all the vegetables and the reserved juice. Add the syrup ingredients and mix well. Cook, uncovered, at a simmer until the vegetables are tender and the liquid is reduced, about 1½ hours. If relish becomes too dry, add a little water or the vegetable juice. Seal in sterile jars. Yield: approximately 4 pints

<u>UNCOOKED FRESH RELISH</u>

Ingredients:

- ½ small head of cabbage

- 1 large sweet onion

- 1 small green pepper

- 1 large, slim cucumber

- 1 large cooking apple

- 2 to 4 tablespoons coarse salt

- Syrup ingredients:

- 2 cups cider vinegar

- 1 cup brown sugar

- 1 teaspoon celery seed

- 1 teaspoon mustard seed

- ¼ teaspoon cloves

- ¼ teaspoon allspice

Directions

1. Prepare the vegetables. Trim and cut the cabbage into pieces. Peel and coarsely chop the onion. Wash the pepper, cut in quarters, remove the seeds, and chop coarsely. Peel the cucumber, cut in quarters lengthwise, remove the seeds, and cut into small pieces. Peel, core, and cut the apple into small pieces.

2. Mix the vegetables and grind. Mix in the salt and let stand overnight in a bowl, covered.

3. In a pan large enough to hold the ground vegetables, mix the vinegar, sugar, celery and mustard seed, and spices, bring to a boil, and let stand overnight, covered.

4. The next day, drain and rinse the vegetables, squeez- ing out the water. If too salty, soak in freshwater for 1 hour and drain well. Combine the vegetables and syrup and let stand at room temperature overnight. Place in clean jars and store in the refrigerator.

5. Yield: approximately 2 pints *Note: For more color, use half of a small green pepper and half of a red. Adding some carrot will also give additional color to the relish.

MINUTE RELISH

Ingredients:

- fresh vegetables, as much as you wish

- coarse salt, ¼ teaspoon for each cup of ground

- vegetables

- vinegar, ¼ cup per cup of vegetables

- sugar, brown or white, 1 tablespoon per cup

- spices of your choosing, ½ teaspoon per cup

- garlic powder, cayenne pepper, mustard seed, or celery seed to taste

Directions

1. Select crisp, fresh vegetables and grind coarsely. Drain and measure.

2. Add the other ingredients for each cup of measured ground vegetables. Mix well and store in clean jars or a bowl in the refrigerator. Your yield depends on how many cups of vegetables you grind. This relish is best made in small amounts and used in short time.